PANHANDLE
POET
~solitude~

by
Marc Livanos

Panhandle Poet
~solitude~
copyright ©2015
by Marc Livanos
All rights reserved

TABLE OF CONTENTS

Acknowledgments

To my son Paul J. Livanos whose creative spirit launched my journey of internal examination and differing views. Paul also composed the score for "Eight Ball" which was performed as a choral piece at NYU Steinhardt's Music and Performing Arts Profession on May 19th, 2013. This composition eventually led to the Jerry Jazz Musician site featuring me and my poem "Ferguson," on December 22, 2014

To my son Alexander Livanos whose clear advice and innate wisdom provided the inspiration for many of my poems.

To Jennifer Manis of the Florida Dept. of Environmental Protection whose love of nature and photographic skills are evident on the cover.

A mighty hug to my wife, Maryann, whose praise and endless support got me to dig deep inside and express myself through my poetry.

With special thanks to my publisher, Susan Lewis Books, whose expertise, delicate editorial advice and wealth of information led to the publishing of this chapbook.

Dedication:

To my wife
and best friend,
Maryann,
who has always
supported
my writing.

Introduction

Like so many other Floridians, I came to Florida from somewhere else. I was drawn here to escape northern winters and to enjoy year round boating. Slowly, I became hooked.

This love affair began in 2010, when I left the fast food and hectic pace of the city. I bought a small boat, fishing rod, programmed my presets to classic country and immersed myself with the friendliest of people. The people and land are the fabric of the panhandle. People enjoy each other. We're all drawn to this isolation that gives you the room to think. Folks in this area actually love this place.

The warm weather, sand hills, red bluffs, scrub wood, swamps, remote beaches, stands of old-growth pine forests, unique waters and bays, tannin stained rivers, large birds, rural villages and centuries of rich heritage surround you. Woven into this vibrant tapestry are the clouds and hues portending discovery around each bend. You can almost squint and be present in Lower Alabama. So, journey with me friends, as I relive the tapestry of these surroundings in my poems.

You can read the entire chapbook in one setting, but if you limit your reading to one poem at a time, you too will travel to this lifestyle. So, put your feet on the desk, don a lifejacket, or just reach for a beer.

Reflections

I

Moonshine Visions

My courtyard Buddha
looks right at me,
sipping my latest moonshine.

My moonshine days
are filled with waterfall rays,
looking within and out again.

These ephemeral days
are never far away.
My moonshine instills the calm.

My mind,
once enlightened,
sees everything.

Like a bird that sings,
I am in everything,
re-discovering the humdrum patter of life.

These moonshine days
have earned a special place
in my courtyard.

Heretofore, I shared only with Buddha,
my favorite mug of fiery brew that
fuels imagination.

Until now. Dear reader,
consider this your
invitation to join me.

Cedar House Inn of St. Augustine

To tell a story
told and retold
till it takes hold,
the Cedar House Inn
celebrates the absence
of the outside world.

Its housekeeper,
timekeeper,
illusionist appears,
smiles,
steps back,
beckoning your inner child.

Memories
of boxed games and
casual conversation
invite the calm
and civility
of the simple life.

Squirrels in a nearby courtyard
scuttle and scurry
on gnarled grey cedars
with leathered, cracked, splintered skin
down to the bark,
waiting for their next acorn.

Night slowly falls.
Traffic palls.
The street becomes silent.

Next door, a gray dog barks.
A fountain slowly drips,
sparking vapors that penetrate the soul.

Magical chimes on
mystical verandas create
alternate realms.
Victorian lights glow in a lifetime outpouring
of preservation, grace and continuity
unyielding in its desire to survive.

Patrons slowly navigate to their beds,
fingering furniture, focusing on old time
lights
infused by the wonder of days gone by.
A gentle aura floats all around,
dreamily repeating,

I need to be here.

Dinner with George

Cobblestone streets
bring me to the old inn door of
Savannah's "Pink House."

Passing through the façade,
the greeter beckons me
towards darkened stairs.

Picture rails, hang with old masters,
thick balusters, newels and nosing,
lead me to the upper landing.

A vast ballroom
has scattered tables
adorned with white linens, crystal and silver.

Hospitality, long forgotten, evokes embraces
from the former owners, who entertained
the likes of Oglethorpe, and our nation's
Founder.

Dark spaces,
filled with simple pleasures and gay rhetoric,
festoon this 1771 house.

From dim valances that light shadows.
an aging waiter, in a starched shirt and tails,
slowly approaches.

He proffers

George's menu -
butter beans, tomatoes and stew.

I stare, straining to see
what lies in shadows
lit by amber lights.

My eyes dart
between the dark corners,
era appropriate furnishings and ivy mantels.

I listen,
slowly sipping more wine.
George is present.

Nothing can be heard, yet my head
readies to explode.
His presence reassures me.

I raise another glass
and silently ask,
How do you see the state of our country?

> *I often look*
> *from the clear upper sky*
> *and see this quilt*
> *of pieces and parts*
> *moving us onward.*
> *Our goal is not*
> *victory for one side,*
> *but for mankind.*
> *We are a patchwork,*
> *no part greater than the other.*

Trust in God
and confidently hope
all will yet be well.
I saw what
could only be told
to those too that have seen.

Walking home, thoughts float
as to the spirit in this storied house,
beyond that behind the bar.

Green

Green -
    permeates souls
    nourishes minds
    eclipses concrete images,

    transforms ideals
    fashions mental labyrinths
    reflects friendships,

    rejuvenates memories
    restores youth
    promotes imagination,

    beckons remembrances
    reveals olden days
    portrays nascent ways,

    bares secret gardens
    retreats for solitude
    powers reflection,

    transcends pretenses
    quiets differences
    showcases tranquility, and

    entices safeguarding
    supporters of preservation
    guardians of the environment.

Time
II

Quittin' Time

On my "Baywalker,"
gliding through Pensacola Bay,
civilization turns to solitude.

Nearby cypress knees,
intertwining with gnarled weathered trees,
reach back decades in time.

Haunted by shrieks from
laughing gulls,
the bow pierces the still waters.

Distant dolphins dance,
feasting on a breakfast
of mullet and ladyfish.

In this roux, I break out the fishing gear,
shunning my eyes from yet another brilliant sun,
and set my mind to wondering.

Wayfarer

Pilgrimages -

> trigger deep emotions
> long forgotten,
>
> illuminate memories
> floating sleepily by,
>
> open gateways for
> wandering souls,
>
> harmonize the past
> with the future,
>
> sear images
> of our inevitable end,
>
> beckon us
> to question -

Are we nothing but shadows
dancing in the corner
of our eyes?

Homer's Eyes

What did Homer see?
Barren rocks,
dancing to the stars out of boredom.
A man-child playing at shadows,
a sea of scalloped bays.
Casually, he started telling a tale.
Done that, said the stars.

From Homer's keen mind
rushed out words
telling of wars utter waste.
Harbingers of the sacrifice of a leader's daughter,
sacrilege of an enemy's body,
death of heroes,
years wasted and ways lost.

The stars were stained
by the cruelty of war,
a realization sighted
by a blind person.
Homer gifted
the stars
with a war poem on peace.

Alchemist

So to speak,
it goes like this.
Why <u>not</u> choose me?
said the alchemist.

Are you ready
for your transformation?
Do you see what may be
glimmering before you?

While majestic butterflies
once lived like worms,
<u>don't</u> journey as an alchemist
but as a wanderer unraveling gifts.

For troublesome change lessens, when
seeing treasures already owned.
As alchemists try to change tin to gold,
you lose worries to treasures at home.

So, turn up the volume.
Revel in gifts you own.
Unravel the gold in your abode,
thankful for resources glistening at home.

Rich Man

Elemental forces
stir brown water.
Fish stare.
Clouds blare.

Trees reflect
quiet water.
Life's in a trance.
Silt settles.

A quacking eeriness
rebounds across the bay.
Water flows incessantly.
Birds chase the day.

Feast on times past,
travel with ancients.
See the natural wonder of nothingness.
Embrace calm.

Nature lives in the moment
but can be damned with
lame excuses that
disinherit your soul.

There are no inert treasures
like perks and privileges.
The most valuable resources
are those of the heart.

Old Tree

Old tree, what do you see?
A life worth sharing?

You stand still, while
life revolves round you.

Is there a purpose,
or just a view?

You look to the sky, and
it looks at you.

You see the parts,
but not the whole.

Each part is before you and
makes your world.

You're entrenched in your part but
like the curve of the earth, it's never ending.

This is your part.
This is your life.

Nature's Peace

Nature's peace shines,
kaleidoscoping time.

Magical turns mystical,
embracing irrelevance.

Primordial images float,
ricocheting reality.

Self-importance recedes
vanquishing insecurity.

Time loses significance,
reaching back before self-awareness.

Futility abounds in all,
except finding our place in the universe.

Life's Journey
III

Into the Abyss

Many times reliance is tested
and those present
fail to find His presence
in the unfolding drama.

A drama all too wasteful and needless,
but none unforeseen, mirroring the pattern
of the Gospel where Jesus is utterly defeated
and the defeat becomes a beginning.

Proceeding through that drama
with His teachings, not as a victim,
but rich in impending new evidence
of the care of God.

Facing drama
with His greatness, not yours,
confident in your proceeding
despite all rationale to the contrary.

Finding your part
in that drama
without temptation
to see an unsolvable problem.

Evoking God's direction to St. Paul,
"Rely on Me,"
for there is no abyss so deep
that He is not deeper.

A Father's Love

A mother's love
is never appreciated,
as it does not grow stronger.
She always loves you.

A father's love
is always exaggerated,
as it comes from restraint
and provides the strength to stand alone.

He endures the pain,
works to pay the bills,
and provides a foundation
built on reflection.

His love comes from insight
that steeps within you
slowly showing you normalcy
in the customary ways of the world.

And in the end,
his love chases away
the doubt and disbelief,
so you can stand on your own.

My Dog "Cookie"

Cookie's inner peace
challenges our perception
of our perspective on life.

She's always comfortable
with herself,
never worrying about her core.

Her core is simple,
just love and affection
form her spirit.

We don't know
what makes us comfortable, if
we don't know our core.

We need work on
what's right with us,
not what's wrong.

There's no trick to learn,
once you know
your inner "Cookie."

Toby, the Oblivious

A proud bichon is he
that frowns quite unknowingly.

A noble face,
elegant with grace.

He blinks,
when he thinks,

and eradicates gloom,
when he enters the room.

He's always fine
and never whines.

But if treats aren't on your list,
his attention doesn't exist.

In fact, he never works fast
and always finishes last.

And, from spring to fall,
he does nothing at all.

He won't go against the tide,
and feels better inside.

Some think him odd,
yet smile and nod.

They do not think he belongs,
but are certainly wrong.

No matter what they say,
he doesn't care anyway.

Work
IV

Transom

Colors, shades, hues
form the outline of my trees,
chiming with the slightest breeze.
I look out,
like a caged bird,
wanting not to be bound.

Sunrays gently spread tranquility,
melting stress,
as I stare
capturing the uncapturable.
Years of work led to boredom.
I work all day till dark.

Light flashes.
Phone rings.
Computer screens glow.
Stale coffee wafts.
My eyes wander up
to that transom.

The stand sways.
Bark ripples.
Branches wave,
enticing me
to waiver
and not focus.

Eight Ball

Things go this way and that.
Sideways, too.
TGIF, I'm done.
My 4-leaf clover has come.
My collar is undone.
I'm where I left off.

But, I'm OK.
They call me Mr. Pay.
As I have a card
that can say-
Yeah Yeah
I'm on my way.

TGIF. I need to get bent
cause I don't like to look
into eyes and see gray,
like a swirling herd of zebras
Despair, keeping time, till in the ground.
OMG, 8-ball, you've got it all.

Alms for the Poor

There once was an illiterate worker,
who was the class clown, and
wasted a childhood
watching TV and partying.

He faulted his parents
for not caring,
while others in his class were
studying and getting ahead.

He succumbed
to functionally-illiterate parents
that lived in poverty,
creating low expectations.

He felt isolated,
to be in a situation
with no end in sight,
floundering in his frustration.

Just as he needs ownership of his misfortune,
we need to open our minds
as one day
we too may lose our way.

A Retrospect of Mr. Whatnut

Hot mess – missed the boat.
Whatnut rules a jazzed reality.
What a hoot!

Cluttered views,
full of vulgarity,
were passing for ingenuity.

Articles once important,
but worthy of garage sales,
were displays of shoestring budgets.

Financial achievements,
formerly flaunted,
were clinically cold curiosities.

Blue-blood soirees,
chronicling greed,
were embellishments of the ego.

Kisses of grime,
brimming with zest,
were illuminations of unpleasantness.

Ormolu claw feet with knots of ego,
soaring skyward,
were incapable of affection.

Jam-packed closets of ready-made chic,
lacking love,
were never treasures of the heart.

Ferguson

Whitewalls better,
blackwalls cheaper.
White collar
has fines.
Inner city
does time.

Michael Brown
Trevon Martin,
Eric Green
scream
not fair using color
to judge our crime.

Like wind before thunder
do not blunder
on all being equal
cause a bullet
buys a seat
in the back of the hearst.

Tires get slashed
when others feel inferior.
Best create
a balance,
and all do time
for a similar crime.

Marine

V

Serene Embrace

Primordial images abound
in a slowly draining river,
inhaling egos.

Water never loses its way
roads eventually decay,
leaving great plans in disarray.

Quiet waters reflect havens
free of worries,
silencing anxieties.

Open skies never end
in a blue panache,
spreading sweet serenity.

Egos remain unquenched,
in an emptiness,
beseeching validation.

And as existentialism floats
in this never ending moat,
nature softly whispers -

Let the river guide you.

Banter

Fudge chocolate water
nips at the boat's keel.
Hurry-up gravy dribbles
from the canopy of clouds.

No fast food here.
No hectic pace.
Just nature's spectacle
unseen from home.

No ego-friendly interactions.
No sour-puss expressions.
Unimportant fixations are
without substance here.

Experience nature's hypnotic rhythm
to form staples in your life,
like banter
amongst friends.

Overboard

In the water.
One with the sea.
Joining my congenital twin.

No sound.
Ready for the flash.
Recalling the umbilical cord.

How free.
No regrets.
Trying not to laugh.

Calmness entices.
Follow nearby fish.
Residing in Davey Jones Locker.

The sea claims.
It does not share.
Its welcoming stay ever known.

Reminding all -
we are but visitors
mindful of forever, no more.

The Locker

It feels like a funeral.
Not a sound,
just the howl of Davey Jones.
Destruction all around.

Valleys to the left.
Valleys to the right.
Steering broadside,
affixed to that helm.

Waves ride on deck,
wildly thrusting to leeward.
Desires and reality collide, as
all stand naked.

Davey Jones beckons,
calling over and over -
Your home is prepared inside my locker,
where no one escapes and rapture is mine.

The brutality forces us
to seek refuge
by accepting a watery grave
as a haven.

Why not Davey Jones Locker,
forsaking a landlubber's heaven
tied to surroundings
and society's restraints?

His howl, like sirens,
once heard,
never releases.
His locker awaits.

Empathy

VI

My Aunt Nitsa

Her once brown hair is fading.
Her frame, never tall, is ever more slender.
Her face radiates acceptance.
Her eyes always twinkle.

Like a special gift,
Aunt Nitsa is one of a kind.
She builds relationships
by creating cherished memories.

At home, her son's wife is
blind to his mother's needs.
It's just about them,
taking without caring.

She gave her home,
living in the basement.
She gave her car,
taking the bus.

They never return calls.
Don't even pretend.
Never appreciating,
just criticizing.

She says it's no use letting it upset you,
as it becomes an acid eating at your insides.
Instead, get out of that place
with cheerful words here and sympathetic nods
there.

If something is bothering you,
the problem emanates from you.
She's an example of the words -

If you do not love,
you are not My disciple.

Sowing Our Own Destruction

Repulsed from unbearable situations.
Riddled with torment.
Illegals come with dreams
for a better life.

All of us come from dust.
None better than the other.
Like our ancestors,
they seek work.

Opinionated profilers,
blind to suffering,
create comfort zones and
sow their own destruction.

Open your eyes and see
anger comes from within.
The immigration problem
emanates from you.

For seeds sown in kindness
reap great benefits
in homes
where compassion reigns.

What to do?
When push comes to shove,
give a hand out.
It is the humane thing to do.

Dark Reflections

Recognizing that my faults
are legion,
I exorcise.

Living in a rut
void of light,
I extinguish.

Having no idea
what it's like in another's shoes,
I judge.

Ignoring pleas
of what is wanted or what to do,
I criticize.

Sensing inflexibility as fear
of a different humanity,
I repent.

Waiting for the Bus

There was a lad
bound to a wheelchair.
He could only quiver and scream,
waiting for the school bus outside his home.

He faulted his parents
for being left alone.
Helpless.
Scared to be on his own.

Parents stretched beyond normal limits ask,
Who will help us?
They cope by spewing insanity
on ill-prepared family members.

His body continued to writhe in pain,
as days idled away.
At last,
anger consumed him.

Both parent and child were isolated,
as if floating on a flimsy boat
in the middle of the sea
seeing water all around them.

Still, there are consequences
for nothing more, than being born.

When the Light Goes Out

We do not need a world
without illness,
ridding us of gratefulness.

Gratefulness –
      for work
      that affords shelter and friends
      to nourish my soul,

      for losses
      that give wisdom and kinship
      with those like me,

      for suffering
      that provides empathy
      to help others,

      for dark places
      that lead
      to enlightenment,

      for complications
      that give strength
      to become a conqueror,

      for weaknesses
      that form in my spirit so as
      to testify to my failures,

for changes
as even the sweetest apple
has a tree within it, and

for exigencies
that allow my testament, right now,
of gratitude and true joy for you.

Retirement is...

staring at blue skies
hovering over canopies of clouds
nipping at strands of Spanish moss,

watching flowers in the breeze
meandering through dreams
gleaning much needed introspection,

sitting in the sunlight
hearing echoes
springing from my happy heart,

bending an elbow with "shine"
inhaling the surrounding warmth
exhaling moody thoughts,

slaloming down grassy slopes
recounting hard-won lessons
murmuring words of thankfulness,

flirting with memories gone by
treasuring those nearby
basking in life's simple pleasures.

Previously Published Works

The site www.JerryJazzMusician.com featured Marc Livanos with his poem *Ferguson* on December 22, 2014. The magazine FreeXpresSion featured the author with his poems *Alms for the Poor, Banter, My Dog "Cookie," Moonshine Visions* and *Green* in the December 2014, Volume XXI – Issue 12, pages 3, 6, 7, & 26, FreeXpresSion again featured the author with poems *Dinner with George, Cedar House Inn of St. Augustine,* and *Toby, the Oblivious* in the February 2015, Volume XXII – Issue 2, pages 3, 16 & 17. PKA's Advocate recognized his poem *Toby, the Oblivious* in the Spring Newsletter. The Legend listed the author's published work and included his poem *The Locker* in the February 2015 issue, *Overboard* in the January 2015 issue and *Transom* in the November 2014 issue.

WestWard Quarterly published *Into the Abyss* in the Winter issue - January 2015, and *Cedar House Inn of St. Augustine* in the Spring-March 2015 issue. Zylophone Band, Poetry Journal's Book 11 of 2014 published *Moonshine Visions,* followed by *Cedar House Inn of St. Augustine*. Shemom published *Quittin' Time* in the Winter issue and *Cedar House Inn of St. Augustine* in the Spring issue.

The Poet's Art magazine published *Nature's Peace* and *The River* in the February issue and *My Dog Cookie* and *Rich Man* in the June issue.

The Pink Chameleon on Line published *My Dog Cookie* and *Green* in issue No. 16. Brigitta Geltrich of Creative With Words published *Old Tree* and *Eight Ball* in 2012. *Eight Ball* was performed as a choral piece at NYU Steinhardt's Music and Performing Arts Profession on May 19th, 2013.

Mr. Livanos' technical articles were published in Shipping Digest and Risk Talk.

39487479R00032

Made in the USA
Charleston, SC
11 March 2015